I0482270

How To Leverage More For Less In Your Business

Now 1+1 = Much More

JOHN MILLAR

DEDICATION

I dedicate this book to my mother and father, who
raised me while self-employed. They
taught me to work hard and listen to everyone but to
make my own choices as to what is right
and what is wrong.. and oh, did I mention work hard?

Anyone who tells you to work smart not hard hasn't
ever done it tough and realized that if
you work smart AND hard you will achieve more than
you can possibly dream.

CONTENTS

Acknowledgments   i

1   SYSTEMS & TECHNOLOGY   Pg 1

2   YOUR BUSINESS   Pg 14

   ACTION PLAN

3   ABOUT THE AUTHOR   Pg 17

4   CLIENT TESTIMONIAL   Pg 19

SYSTEMS & TECHNOLOGY

Schedule & Complete Regular Maintenance On All Equipment

Rather than waiting until your machinery crashes, get it serviced in times of low need.

It will also cost you less in the end. Regular routine maintenance not only will keep your machinery running in tip-top condition, it will also save you money by not having to endure costly non-productive downtime. Neglect could also affect your manufacturer's warranties and insurance policies.

Use Computer Invoicing & Credit Monitoring

Save yourself time and money, and be sure that everything is consistent.

Many excellent software packages run everything from invoicing to bank account balances. They are simple to use and consistent. They will also monitor overdue payments and issue statements for you. Use them; they will save you time and money.

Document & Picture All Tasks In An Operations Manual

An Operations Manual includes what needs to be done, when it needs to be done, who should do it, what the standards are and how to measure the results.

This is important, as it not only sets out how each task is to be done, it states what the standards are, what happens when things go wrong and how team members can monitor and measure their progress. Think of the Operations Manual as the definitive guide on how things are done in your business. It is a systematic guide to getting the job done, with illustrations and photographs where applicable.

Run A Computerized Stock Control System

Do not leave stock control to chance. You can do with one computer what five or six people used to do.

Stock control is one area of your business that lends itself to computerization. Tie in everything from ordering stock, pricing, and stock replenishment to inventory control into the same system. Make sure you run on the "Just in Time" stock purchasing principle – it could not be easier. In addition, it is more accurate.

Complete Systems Training & An Orientation Program

Training people how to use a good system takes about a tenth of the time it takes to teach people how to do the job.

Remember, systems run the business and people run the systems. Train them how to run the systems and your business will flourish. Start training your people right from the beginning by including system's training in the orientation program. That way you can establish a systems culture in your business.

Use The Latest Computer Programs

Updates to software often result in better features, fewer bugs and greater productivity.

It is all about consistency. There is nothing worse than not being able to use certain software packages or not being able to open a simple document just because you are running outdated software. Being up-to-date also sends out a positive message about your company.

When you install a new software package, it is a prime opportunity to hold a training session. This also serves as a good strategy for team building.

Complete A Phone/Fax Systems Upgrade

Technology saves you so much time when you use it well.

Moreover, in business time is money. Having the latest technology may also be more cost effective. Often, one new piece of equipment takes the place of three older pieces. It will work better and you will experience less down time. Very often, they are easier to use and take up less space in the office. Be sure to consider ISPN lines or convert to mobile phones.

Go Through & Regularly Update Quality Control/Assurance

Once you document everything, it is just a matter of following through.

Things change over time. Systems and procedures are reviewed and amended to suit changing conditions and requirements. Be sure to reflect these changes in your quality control or assurance manuals or procedures. It is simple, but easily overlooked.

Run A Computer Back Up System

This can save a mountain of time should the worst happen to your computers.

Computers can and do crash and they usually do so at the most inconvenient time. Losing all of your data is not only infuriating it can cost you everything. Having a backup system can be extremely simple – it can be as easy as getting your people to transfer their files or data onto disk at the end of each day. There are many sophisticated systems available, ranging from downloads onto tape to the automatic transfer of information across the Internet to a safe remote site each evening. Either way, you must back up your information.

Run Both Internal & External E-Mail

As long as people do not go crazy, it will save you mountains of time and energy.

Sending information internally via e-mail is efficient, fast and inexpensive. It is far less expensive than distributing office memos or letters. In addition, the sender knows it has been delivered. There is also an electronic record of it, so it saves storage space as well. You can set up an "all staff" email group to make distribution simple. You can also establish department groups, groups that run on seniority lines, or you can send e-mails to individuals.

Document & Chart All Work-Flow Processes

You have to know what follows what, and where everything should go next. Then it is easy to write "how to".

Drawing up a flowchart of your various work processes will help you to clearly understand the mechanics of your business. It will assist in pinpointing bottlenecks and things that could be done better and easier. It will also assist new team members to get on their feet more quickly and to help everyone be more productive.

Document All Sales & Marketing Systems

If it worked, then it is a system you want to keep using.

It is no good running a sales and marketing system that does not work. It also does not make sense to run a system you are not sure works. Document every successful sales and marketing effort so it can be repeated again and again. This will lead to consistency and save you time and money as it brings in results.

Document Information Flow Process

If it is documented, it will have to go somewhere and eventually someone will have to process it. Record where each piece of paper goes, and then anyone in your business can process it.

There is no point having cupboards full of reports and memos if nobody ever makes use of them. Cluttered shelves and drawers are a waste of time and money. Understanding the flow of information in your business is crucial to running a good business. Document its flow path and save everyone time and heartache. You will be more organized and so will your people and your business.

Use A Purpose-Designed Computer Database Program

Manage your customers, their buying patterns and your business through your computer.

It is as simple as that. Create a database (there are several excellent sales management products on the market), starting with all your leads, and develop from there. Include names and contact details as well as information relating to their buying behaviour and patterns. This information will become the central core of information for your business. It will be priceless. Use it to easily increase your profit.

Network All Computers For Ease Of Access

File sharing, printer sharing and running a

networked system means you only have to change it once.

Networks make sharing information simple and efficient. It also saves money, as there is no longer a need to print out documents to pass around. You can save on the number of peripheral printers and fax machines you need to run. Instead of running many medium quality printers, you can run a good quality laser printer that is connected to all computers through the network. In addition, when it comes to updates, you only need to do this once, as everyone on the network will automatically have access to it.

Use Rosters & Schedules For Repetitive Tasks

By focusing on the routine being done without anyone really noticing, you are then able to focus on the customer.

Nobody likes doing repetitive tasks, but unfortunately, they still need to be done. Spread them around. That way everyone shares a lighter load. If everyone takes a turn at doing it, each person might only get the cleaning duties once a month, but that is better than some person having to do it three times a day, every day. You will also be emphasizing the importance of teamwork.

Complete A Policies & Procedures Manual

If everything is written down then duplication is a simple step, and you are reliant on the system, not the people.

The key to developing a successful business is to develop a set of systems that runs the business. Systems ensure things run smoothly, every time. The systems are recorded in a set of manuals, known as policy and procedure manuals. They are the main reference books for the business.

Complete A Machinery Automation & Upgrade

If it does the job a whole lot better and faster, then it is probably less expensive and more reliable in the end.

Remember that machinery needs to be maintained and upgraded from time-to-time. Build this into your system and review it regularly. Technological advances provide benefits that include the automation of various tasks as well as cost savings and better levels of precision. Are you missing out?

Document All Accounting Systems

It is far better to have a system and an unskilled person than a highly skilled person who may leave at any minute.

Accounting systems are easy to use, once set up. Everyone can also use them – much of the data input can come from other interacting systems such as sales and marketing, inventory, purchasing and operations. If your accounting system is well-designed and documented, anyone should be able to use it.

Upgrade Office Equipment Regularly

If upgrading office equipment is going to assist in productivity, then you are probably saving and not spending.

Having the latest in office equipment not only assists in being more efficient, it makes your people feel good as well. Morale is better and productivity is higher. It is also good for your image.

Prioritize Extraordinary Tasks

Extraordinary tasks can be time-consuming and costly to deal with. Can your system cope?

Prioritize extraordinary tasks as they occur. Get them sorted out as soon as possible and do not forget to upgrade your systems and manuals accordingly. Use these as team building exercises if possible. They can be carried out during slack periods or after hours depending on their nature. If extraordinary tasks happen regularly, revisit your systems and fine tune where necessary.

Re-system As Your Company Grows

As your company grows, your systems may be tested to the limit of their original design, rendering them outdated, inefficient or unable to cope. They may no longer be relevant and workable.

Review and audit your systems as your business grows. It is far easier amending or adapting a system as you grow rather than starting from scratch and developing a completely new system to cater for a very different set of circumstances.

Security Systems

How secure is your business? Can it survive a major robbery or even a computer crash?

Theft, industrial espionage and petty theft are becoming major problems for business owners the world over. What would you do if you were the target of an organized gang? What would you do if your computer network were infected with a debilitating computer virus? Are these possibilities managed by your security system? Conduct regular audits and consult with external professionals to ensure you are not at risk. Discuss options with your insurance company, fire department and police service (if applicable).

Print Your Company's Vision Statement

Write out why you are in business, and your own personal standards. Include a summary of your ethics, and an outline of how you deal with customers. This is your compass that directs your team's shared goals. Where are you going? What is essential to you? What will be reflected in your company? How will it be perceived? How does it operate? What does it value and believe? Then give it to every client – it will blow them away.

Even better, get a local print shop to design and

print it. Have your vision statement professionally mounted and then hang it in clear view of your customers. This way you will have the chance to demonstrate your high level of professionalism. If people believe that you are professional, they will be more inclined to do business with you.

Company Profile

This can work as a serious sales tool – you create a five to six page document detailing what makes your company so great. More importantly, talk about why your company is the best choice for the prospect – and what you plan to do for them! A company profile can give the consumer confidence in you, particularly if you have just opened your business in a new area. Let people know what your history is, and where you company is headed. If you explain the benefits of dealing with your company, you are sure to get extra sales.

Organizational Chart

You have a team playing the game of business. Would you play any other game without everyone understanding the position of each player on the team? Regardless of how simple and straightforward you think your business structure is, consider the young employee just starting their life in business. People with experience who join your organization come with the organizational structure of previous employers in their mind. Ensure they know how your company works. It is not enough to tell people how things work, letting them see the structure of your organization is more important. "A picture is worth a thousand words." Team communication is one of the underlying principles of a great company.

Opening, Closing - Daily Checklist

Creating routines that can be followed by everyone from the first day they come to work for you is a real time saver and reduces the frustration many people have when training new Team Members. Remember that this is your team – the more complete the playbook is the more effective the Team. One of the spin-off benefits of something this basic is that it sets a professional mind set with new hires. They can see right from the outset that detail is important in your business.

YOUR BUSINESS
ACTION PLAN

How To Leverage More For Less In Your Business

Priority	Task	Individual Responsible	Investment	Start Date	Complete Date
	Systems & Technology				
High-Moderate-Low	Schedule & Complete Regular Maintenance On All Equipment				
High-Moderate-Low	Use Computer Invoicing & Credit Monitoring				
High-Moderate-Low	Document & Picture All Tasks In An Operations Manual				
High-Moderate-Low	Run A Computerized Stock Control System				
High-Moderate-Low	Complete Systems Training & An Orientation Program				
High-Moderate-Low	Use The Latest Computer Programs				
High-Moderate-Low	Complete A Phone/Fax Systems Upgrade				
High-Moderate-Low	Go Through & Regularly Update Quality Control/Assurance				
High-Moderate-Low	Run A Computer Back Up System				
High-Moderate-Low	Run Both Internal & External E-Mail				
High-Moderate-Low	Document & Chart All Work-Flow Processes				
High-Moderate-Low	Document All Sales & Marketing Systems				
High-Moderate-Low	Document Information Flow Process				
High-Moderate-Low	Use A Purpose-Designed Computer Database Program				
High-Moderate-Low	Network All Computers For Ease Of Access				

JOHN MILLAR

Priority	Task	Individual Responsible	Investment	Start Date	Complete Date
High-Moderate-Low	Use Rosters & Schedules For Repetitive Tasks				
High-Moderate-Low	Complete A Policies & Procedures Manual				
High-Moderate-Low	Complete A Machinery Automation & Upgrade				
High-Moderate-Low	Document All Accounting Systems				
High-Moderate-Low	Upgrade Office Equipment Regularly				
High-Moderate-Low	Prioritize Extraordinary Tasks				
High-Moderate-Low	Re-system As Your Company Grows				
High-Moderate-Low	Security Systems				
High-Moderate-Low	Print Your Company's Vision Statement				
High-Moderate-Low	Company Profile				
High-Moderate-Low	Organizational Chart				
High-Moderate-Low	Opening, Closing - Daily Checklist				

ABOUT THE AUTHOR

John Millar is the Managing Director, Senior Business Coach Trainer and Consultant with More Profit Less Time Pty Ltd and CEO-ONDEMAND. Along with his many other business interests, John is proud to have been an associate of the most successful coaching team in the world.

He is recognized as a global leader and has been benchmarked against over 1,300 colleagues in 31 countries. John has over 25 years of hands-on ownership, management, coaching, and entrepreneurial experience in a broad range of industry sectors, including retail, wholesale, import, export, IT, trades and trade services, automotive, primary production, food services, transport, manufacturing, mining, professional services, the fitness industry, and more.

He has extensive experience developing and providing training for small to medium-sized companies and a variety of publicly listed corporate companies. John is an accomplished and talented public and professional speaker. He has been a mentor working with sales/management activities for businesses with a turnover under $100,000 per annum, over $100 million turnover, and everything in between, with great success.

John currently works with business owners and their teams across Australia and has a "Whatever it takes" attitude that has enabled him to help his clients grow their business profits by up to 800%.

If you are ready to be coached by one of the best in the business, register at:

www.ceo-ondemand.com.au

Make sure to visit www.moreprofitlesstime.com for the new online Management Development Program: The Business Essentials Series.

ACCLAIM FOR JOHN MILLAR'S BUSINESS COACHING AND TRAINING IN THEIR OWN WORDS...

"Without John Millar as my Business Coach I wouldn't have a business today."—Grant Jennings Managing Director, Jigsaw Projects

"Taking the decision to be coached and trained by John Millar was carefully considered after experiencing those who over promised and under delivered. I am pleased to say the content of his courses are the tools we all need to master as business owners. His delivery is engaging, thought provoking and empowering and after every session l came away re-energised. John always makes himself available for business building advice both via Skype and face to face beyond the scope of delivery. With his extensive personal experience in building small businesses, he knows and understands what it takes to establish and grow a business.I have no hesitation endorsing John Millar as an educator and business coach and the bonus is he is a very nice person."— Anne Lederman Managing Director FB Salons"

Johns training with my management team was excellent, it was very different from the business coaching and support I have had in the past. John was clear, thoughtful and he addressed the issues we needed to cover without us even knowing they were being addressed! His follow up has been fantastic and exactly what I needed. I would recommend John and his team to anyone looking at getting some business coaching and training done" —Wendy Crawford, Peopleworx

"In my dealings with John as our business coach, I have found him to be a motivated and insightful agent of positive change. He is able to burrow down to the root cause of issues and introduce effective forms of measurement. John then identifies and implements practical solutions and is there to provide the gentle persuasion required to ensure that results are achieved." —Mark Felton, Lindale Insurances

"You have coached and trained us so well throughout the year that we are now used to & find it easy to prepare a 90 day plan, then breaks it down to actionable bite size pieces. Planning in business & personal life certainly is important. It allows us to identify the important things & the bigger picture.

Thank you for your support & guidance throughout the year. And not to mention your insight, external perspective to review & assist our business moving forward." —Linda Turner, Director Roy A McDonald Certified Practicing Accountants

"If you want to achieve sales results you never thought were possible and give yourself a competitive edge my strong suggestion is to engage John services and listen closely to what John has to say, during the time I was trained by John I was one of eight sales consultants in a national business for 10 out of the 13 months I lead the sales tally and in 1 quarter I generated three times the revenue of the national sales force combined. Johns training and experience was well worth the investment and paid big dividends. Thanks John." —Julian Fadini, Bellvue Capital

"John is a very enthusiastic trainer and business coach, he is very passionate about getting business owners and their team where they need to be. He goes the extra mile to keep ahead of the latest developments which he then uses to benefit his clients." —Darren Reddy CPA

"I have been to a few seminars and heard John speak numerous times about sales, marketing and business. He is a very knowledgeable and extremely enthusiastic business coach in all his interactions and I would recommend him to all business owners who need a sales and marketing boost!" —Andrew Heath, Managing Director, Fresh Living Group

"I worked with John Millar and found his business knowledge, passion and innovation to be inspiring. He has always been able to set (and achieve) strategic long and short-term goals both for himself and his clients without losing that personal connection he builds with everyone he meets. He has been and I believe will continue to be a strong mentor and trainer for anyone wanting to take that next step in their business." —Bree Webster, Online Marketing Guru

"Massive Action Day" – what an understatement, John Millar's 4 hour frenzy challenged me to seriously review areas of my business I would not have gone to …. In this way, the process identified incongruence's in my mind, my business and my modus operandi. It's created a paradigm shift. Thanks John, the road map just got a whole lot clearer. Your friendship and insights since 2003 have been a gift to my business and I." —Andrew Reay, Counsellor, Hypnotherapist and Counsellor, Thinkshift Transformations

"John Millar is not your usual Business coach or trainer; he gets involved with you and your business and provides hands on help to make sure you follow through on his advice. He is highly motivated to help his clients and his personal guarantee certainly shows this. He has now transposed his thoughts, advice and love of good business onto a series of DVD's in his business venture – More Profit Less Time. This has excellent tips and advice for anyone either starting out or already in business. I highly recommend John to any business owner who wants to run a business and not a j.o.b.!" —Darren Cassidy, Managing Director HR2U

"I and many of my Business Partners and colleagues have worked with John since 2010 as our business oath, trainer and motivator and found him to be an extremely motivational person to assist us achieve our business goals. This company and its products allows for John's skill set to be accessed by a wider number of potential clients. His very professional DVD series is extremely good value for money and is easily accessible for all of us who are time poor. If you are looking to maximise your and your business's results and to start achieving your goals and dreams, contact John; you won't look back!!" —Mark Cleland, Mortgage Choice

"John develops real relationships with the people he comes into contact with. He is passionate about what he does. His DVD and group training series, is full of good ideas and process to make your business better. Knowing what to do and actually doing it are two different things. John is excellent at helping you get things done." —Carey Rudd, Sales Director, Online Knowledge

"I have known John since 2004 and found him to be extremely knowledgably in both Sales and Business systems as a business coach without peer. John has provided me with business advice as well as personal coaching over the years, helping me with the running of my organisation. I'm impressed with John's DVD series where he has condensed a lot of the information in an easy to follow format that any business owner can use immediately. I wish he had released these DVDs earlier, as they are a goldmine of information, and practical how to that allow anyone to increase the profit in their business and get back valuable wasted time." —Steve Psaradellis, Managing

Director, TEBA

"John's DVD and workbook delivery of his no-nonsense advice provides a low-cost option for those business owners looking to set and achieve goals that will increase profit. I found the conversational style of the DVD's easy to follow, whilst the requirement to pause the DVD and write down some action points ensured a level of commitment to the advice being provided." —Mark Felton, Lindale Insurances

"I only met John briefly at a BNI meeting and knew instantly i need to hire him for my business as my business coach. His attitude towards work and how to improve my cash line had an instant effect on before, even before I finally hired him on an official basis. I found myself thinking "what would John do" and this was only after just meeting him. I cannot see my business expend and give me "More Profit Less Time" without John's expert direction and training. If you want to succeed in business life, you need John Millar, without him you're just kidding yourself " — Leslie Cachia, Managing Director, Letac Drafting

"I can highly recommend John Millar to any business owner who wants to grow his business. When I hear very positive feedback from colleagues who are skeptics by nature about John's ability and skills, I know John will help all those he comes in contact with. John comes with a selfless nature and the willingness to work inside a client's business to make it succeed. Rare indeed!" —Darren Cassidy, Managing Director, HR2U"I first met John Millar in mid-2010 and have always found him to be of an honest and generous character that engenders an easy association with him. I love how easy he is to listen to and how passionate he is about his work and topics. John demonstrates a love for life and his work and I have no hesitation in recommending his services." —Kathie M Thomas, Managing Director, VA

"I have listened to John speak on a number of occasions and find him a very knowledgeable speaker with a passion for what he does. I have also interacted with a number of his clients and they all tell me that he helps them achieve results in their business. If you are looking for business help John is a person you can trust." —Carey Rudd, Sales Director, Online Knowledge

"John knows his stuff, he knows how the get results, John has so many great ideas in building a business and helping business owners work less and make more money. John has released a DVD set on doing just that. I have watched the 1st one and it was great, very informative and easy to understand, I happily recommend John to anyone in need of help and guidance" —Frank Eramo, Proprietor, Dynotune

"I have known John only for a short time, however the impact that he has had on me, not just my business has helped me to visualise opportunities that I began to doubt my ability to realise. He is encouraging and at the same time challenging so that he can/you can, begin to see how to maximise the business potential, John calls it being an unreasonable friend, I call it being a mate. If you have any questions about the direction of your business, if you want to seem your bottom line improve not just turnover but real profit, if you want a person who will work with you then I strongly recommend that you engage him at your earliest convenience. John is the best thing that has happened to my business. I could tell you about the way he is on track to make 1/2 a million for me on his contacts alone, but that actually sells him short, he has become like my partner in business, and cares about my success as if it was his own, we will flourish because I took the step to employ his training to help me grow. If you get a chance to get him training you, don't wait like I did, get in as quickly as possible, his time is your business and if like me your business is to make money, then every day you don't have him on retainer you lose money." —Russell Summers, Managing Director, The Give Life Centre

"It's usually easy to be mediocre in business but it's impossible when you have John Millar training you. He has been my right hand since 2003!" —David Manser, CFO, Hydrosteer

"I now have a commercial, profitable business and now it's my choice when I work IN my business and when I work ON it and have had john helping me in business since 1988. I can't imagine not having John as a part of our business." —David Wall, Director, D&K Transport

"The work John has done since 2008 coaching and training our marketing team, administration and finance teams, buyers, store managers and staff nationally have been fantastic." —Ross Sudano, Director, Anaconda Adventure Stores

"John is a creative, professional, practical and committed business coach and trainer. His approach since we first met him in 1994 to working with a client team through the application of useful tools, information and anecdotes along with his easy going & easy to understand delivery sets him apart from other business coaches that I have used in the past." —Anthony Beasley, Director, The Astra Group

"I have worked with John Millar for the since 2004 and I didn't think it was possible to achieve what we have achieved together. His business coaching, training and services just get better and better!" — Terrance Chong, Managing Director, Echo Graphics and Printing

"John's business coaching, training and support has transformed our business across Australia and New Zealand since 2008."—rose vis, managing director, VIP Australia

"We first met John in 2005, he is AMAZING at sales, marketing, operations, logistics, finance training and so much more. Since engaging John as our business coach our business has exploded, our team are happy, our clients are raving about us and my husband and I now take at least 12 weeks holidays a year, EVERY year." —Shirley Du, Director, Goldline Technology

"It's the no nonsense results driven business coaching and training focus John bought to the table that had such a massive effect on our business." — David Runkel, Director, Tracomp Fabrication and Steel

"We started working with John in early 2010, within 90 days of working with and being trained by John Millar we had the biggest and most profitable month in our 15 year history. That's impressive." —Hugh

Gilchrist, Managing Director, Australian Moulding Company

"If you don't have John as your business trainer you aren't meeting your business potential." —Don Robertson, Director, Medallion Electrical Services

Thank You!